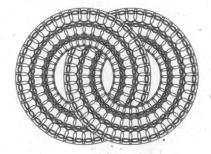

Rise Wildly

Rise

Wildly

TINA KELLEY

CAVANKERRY
PRESS

CavanKerry Press Ltd.
Fort Lee, New Jersey
www.cavankerrypress.org

Publisher's Cataloging-In-Publication Data
(Prepared by The Donohue Group, Inc.)
Names: Kelley, Tina, author.
Title: Rise wildly / Tina Kelley.
Description: First Edition. | Fort Lee, New Jersey : CavanKerry Press, 2020.
Identifiers: ISBN 9781933880808
Subjects: LCSH: Interpersonal relations—Poetry. | American poetry—21st century. | LCGFT: Poetry.
Classification: LCC PS3611.E443253 R57 2020 | DDC 811/.6—dc23

Cover artwork: Judith Bergerson
Cover and interior text design by Ryan Scheife, Mayfly Design
First Edition 2020, Printed in the United States of America

CavanKerry Press is grateful for the support it receives from the New Jersey State Council on the Arts.

Also by Tina Kelley

to my friends, who sustain me

Contents

1.

2.

3.

4.

5.

1.

I Wish You Had Known, When You Launched Me

how I loved my home pond, its aerated, bleachy smell,
the beech leaves around it, the skating, picnics,
scout ceremonies, my kids visiting now,

how I would feel at home in the sky, climbing high hills,
seeing bluegrass like tails of galloping horses
slowed down, like cirrus clouds sped up.

I wish you could know I buckled up every single time,
fell for a Miró painting called *The Diamond Smiles*
at Twilight, never walked into a bar alone.

Could you guess I'd marry the kind of man who shared,
who gave great advice on what car to buy?
Did you have any idea I'd have a kid

who'd say "do you think I shouldn't like you as much as I do,
being a teenager and all?" I hope you could hope
that, yes, I was meticulously raised,

that a friend would call me serene, that I got so old my scars faded,
and I learned of 100,000 undersea mountains,
only a thousand of them named.

Did the smallest thought of yours guess
how very much I would
love it here?

Why I Cried Reading This at Liss and James's Wedding

—not just because I was pregnant
—but because the last line was hers

Some people fall in love just around the edges. For others
love is fireworks in fog, true grandeur unrecognized,
password never guessed, beautiful torture missed.
For Melissa, for James, it's immersion, discovery, engagement.

The sign outside the psychic's read Today Only, Readings $10.
We didn't believe her; the sign was not painted for use on just one day.
But Today Only is a lucky charm. Time, peaceful as tap water, begins now,
poured into one glass to sustain you, today only and another day and more.

You'll be kind to one another, and he'll bring laughter home.
You'll build the peace of the household, and she'll amaze you with wit.
He is anchor and oxygen. She is voluptuous and volatile, diving under
together, bravely, to see a freshly-washed-window view of the world.

Today Only is that jubilant moment when you finally hit the jelly
in the center of the donut and stand together shining in that wide,
united way a diamond throws light. A carpenter builds a deck and view,
a pond in the back, with a waterfall. May you be a perfectly ripe pear,

"yielding to gentle pressure," a sure sign of readiness. Carry on, gently,
and you will find a carriage ride, a sweet old Ford pickup, a hammock, a sea.

Planting, Nearest the Prayer

You, new garden, have all the charms of a seven-month-old baby.
You sit up and smile, stay where I put you for a few short weeks.
You haven't confounded me yet. I haven't fallen behind, failed,
or felt regret. See "verve," "new ambition." See "various hopes."

What tricks will you do? Attract bees, give me edible blue flowers
to freeze in ice cubes, produce blooms for each room and for hanging
from attic rafters, herbs for a summer of dishes, seed heads for finches
in the fall. I'm curious, what will thrive and reseed and naturalize,

which will the squirrels eat, the drought singe, the trees overshade?
With compost from three years of dinners, night crawlers from the bin,
not-yet-severed soaker hose dug in to bathe roots, you may turn marvelous.

I want to sit with you, parse the evening birdsong, feel the spring rinsing,
the possibility of jewels, ever unmined, miles deep under the ocean floor.
My wine, you erase the thump in the gut, turn me capable, full, and desired.

On a Record James Agee Recites from Memory His Poems, Auden's, Shakespeare's, Etc.

Here is where it hits me in the heart—
the Lord's Prayer. I have said it, in bed,
forever, twenty thousand times. I have heard
close-cropped Episcopalians, tall in suits
behind me say the words, some theatrically,
some to hide with the voice-wind around us.

But to hear him pray it, his voice less boisterous
and Southern than I'd expected, that "gain"
in "against us" more British, is to come too close,
to wedge beneath his breath, to touch, be touched
too deep: a kiss in the ear, a whisper of God's home
number. I shouldn't think this way about a dead man,
a married one at that, but dead is not a word for him.

Not while letters form words.

The Brother My Parents Almost Adopted

I almost grew up with a man in this world,
but my father had a major heart attack
right before the baby boy was supposed to arrive
from Maine I think. Cipher baby, a circumstance
miscarriage, someone for my mother to mourn?

I can look at any 54-year-old American male and wonder,
are you adopted? Did we almost share a childhood, a life?
I'm sure he grew up somewhere, maybe with a sister.
Maybe he passed southbound on the highway as we headed up
to Lake Winnepesaukee once, a red Toyota Camry doing 55,
just across the median strip.

If Dad's artery hadn't jammed shut
that August, we would've known each other
more completely than anyone knows us.
I could've had someone to ask why the folks
acted strange some days. I could've questioned
authority sooner. I might've learned better how to argue,
seeing father-son head-butting.

He would've pulled my orbit into an oval, made me share the spotlight
and dessert more. I could've learned the art of protective sweetness.
Mom could've spread her skills around, not focused solely on me, hurrah!
Dad could've had grandchildren sooner, seen his surname live on. A brother
might've helped visit Ma, clean out her apartment, and notarize forms.

Oh, my kids could have an uncle.
I miss someone faceless, scentless,
someone no one I know has ever met,
or if they did, how would I know?
No one knows my childhood but me.

Vitamin Awe

awe, measured in two different ways, was the strongest
predictor of lower levels of [proteins associated with stress].

—Emotion, *a journal of the American Psychological Association, 2015*

For life-lasting doses: trip to Yosemite; hike up Horseshoe Canyon
at dusk for gilt clouds, best pictures; storm at the rocky beach, otters feeding.

Once-ever moments, the bald eagle over Route 10. A shiny black car
tagged DECEIT, passing on the right. Nashville warbler on the roof in Seattle,

saw-whet owl perched on the fence by the Newark bureau. How to measure it?
In postcards, inches, palpitations per minute, cc's of happy tears?

In self-reports from college freshmen. How to find awe? At the golden hour.
A half a cup from the travel brochure. The son dancing to fire's rhythm.

Watching, with binoculars, the purple finch sing. Play me music soaring
so high I dread death. Show me the old songwriter playing her guitar's dreams.

I'll fix some lemon tea, spend time with the fresh thoughts of the astronomer,
his theory of "a cyclic bouncing universe," of another Big Bang

next Thursday, another beetle species discovered before dying out,
an hour to smell jasmine and knit, the yarn something shiny for my fingers.

Adding a New Heartbeat

I have seen that color in the buds on the trees,
that color that reminds me of blood but is not blood,
spring but not spring. It travels north fifteen miles a day.
All I want to do is meet this creature inside me,

know if it is a son, another daughter, but if I met it today
it would die. It must stay till the light lasts longer,
till the trees bud out, till first fireflies and womb weather,
when heat and humidity outside match in.

So I watch goldfinches ripen, brighter than dandelions,
brighter than new tennis balls, brighter each day
from eating blackest thistle seed. Just two weeks ago
grayish brown, dull as females. Now, almost Easter.

When they are brighter than first lightning bugs perhaps.
When honeysuckle blooms. Honey and suckling.
If we get deep enough away to hear the wood thrush,
maybe then you will be ready for my gift, your birth.

Getting Through the A's in *Angels: Their Names and Meanings*

There are angels for inserting the soul into the body at birth,
angels who invented carousels and all the new French fashions.
There's one just for the 26th of each month, for honey, sexuality.
Aban is your guardian ten months before death; another protects

fifth children. In heaven's meadows upon meadows, one angel
governs confusion, one does nothing at all till armageddon,
one rules warm winds. The keeper of fiery triplicities seduces
the regent of Wednesdays, and they're all new every morning,

born through every godbreath, created by each fresh human sin.
They crochet cotton breasts for cancer survivors, telling corny jokes.
They feather insights to the bored, quietly advise on paint colors.
One's pregnant with death, one protects kinglets, but none felt like

mine until I spotted a green sea turtle, blunt and kindly, slowly
lifting its arms in hosannas to the quicksilver surface shining down.

2.

Watching My Father Watch His Widow

Remember how powerless we were in our dreams,
doll, seeing the baby fall but unable to catch her?
We tried to cry out but were muted, merely groaning.
It is fifty times more frustrating now.

I saw you struggle to move the truck seat forward,
child bride, five years younger, foot shorter. I saw
you flush the nitroglycerin pills, silently cursing
my constant need of them, and their failure.

Gad, when do you need a good man more than now,
with your shooting leg pains, backbone arthritis,
dizziness, tiny shards of sleep if the ledger's off?
Damned old age: *rallentando*, without the glory.

Sweetheart, don't fret so, that you missed my last words.
I've forgotten them. But I still have that blood-deep need
to help you up from the low chair, pour you a drink,
make you laugh. Husbands are wasted on the young.

The Fetal Fawn inside the Roadkilled Deer

In the dark alive,
I hear water against land.
I hear undersides of rain.

The giant jolt, the twisted spine.
How long will cold keep sharpening?
I am, but the darkness knows me not.

Grope without hands. Push without goal.
Leaden walls stiffen. Dust settles on sea,
past the barbed-wire finish line.

Her absence is blank presence,
plain, tall mausoleum, benthic.
Our spirits haunt each other—boat

with brown sail, sailor's stale eye.
Wind sounds like turning in sleep.
I am blown blind, a firework dud.

The tough, fried cornmeal husk on my heart
would melt if I could just stumble and run,
these hours between death and a burial.

The blood color of eyelids facing sun,
fading. Fluid congeals. I declare
myself gone, cold.

The 87th Easter

She wanted to get up
for the standing ovation,
but that would've meant
me climbing over her,
urging her arms around
my waist, hauling her up,
and we were in the back
of the theater. She couldn't
applaud in that position,
so I sat next to her and
clapped hard and felt bad.

But the next day, when
the organ started the first
hymn, Jesus Christ, ris'n
today, she reached for
the pew in front of her.
I was glad this still meant
enough to her, and lifted.
I wedged my thigh beneath
her, held my arm around her,
hoped she didn't feel me trembling.

"I'm Having the Death I'd Always Hoped For"

in gratitude for Gus Lindquist, 86, an artist in town

His voice from intensive care
sounded chipper, very much his:
"Hey! I'm pulling the plug today."
I inhaled, asked if he wanted a visit.
I had to get my son from school first.
Gus would try to last that long.

At the hospital, I found him
comfortable, curious, fascinated.
Unafraid of earplug silence, darkness,
focused on creativity, diversity, love.
He wanted the young doctor's company,
told her, after a few calls and emails
on his to-do list, to please stop dialysis.

It would take a day.
He wouldn't suffer.
I stayed an hour,
kissed Gus goodbye.
The cheek was cold.

Walking down the hall
I didn't crumble. Off
to my son's soccer game,
somehow. By next morning
his heart slowed to done.

I couldn't say rest in peace.
In an ancient ritual he knew,
one shines light on the other's
head, heart, and hands. Rest in light.

The Hill Looks Steeper, the Two Maples Gone

There is a pang there that makes poetry.

—Robert Frost, on his house in New Hampshire

We visited every Sunday, moved in with Unc after Granny died. When we left
twenty years later, the buyer loved the place, told us which rooms each kid chose.
Right after the closing he brought blueprints to the township for a giant mansion,
cut the house down the middle, crushed the 1740 rooms, left the hall naked to rain.

The hall where I heard Dad fall. The hall where he didn't get up. The hall he left.
Brown leaked on gold wallpaper, the steps from my bedroom hung over nothing.
Homesickness doubled for half a house, the staircase from Frost's "Home Burial,"
the farmhouse from *The Good Earth,* Amityville mansion in my mind. Backdoor,

where Chuck left the Easter cake and rang the bell and sprinted away. Pantry,
where short Mr. Van Scythe drowned in the pickle barrel during a long-ago party.
Yard where I hung laundry, feeling like a sieve blown clear of leaves and seeds.
Driveway my bachelor uncle ambled down at dusk, whistling "Beautiful Dreamer."

I'll never again be in a family that lives in one place sixty years. But in the field, look,
the dreamed-of beehives, father-daughter ritual smelling of cottonwood and smoke.

The Dying in Slow Motion, The Woman Who Taught Me to Knit

The diminishing yarn ball dances out in fast joy
if I know I have more hanks, feel momentum,
see a landmark reached. No extra skeins here,
85-degree apartment, steady loss, new phrases
to measure it: "Mechanical soft/nectar thick" diet.
"Sponge pops" for oral hygiene, to clean those
buccal folds, between teeth and cheek, when
swallowing falters. Clean mouth reduces risks
of "aspiration pneumonia" (but wasn't to aspire
to hope?) if she chokes and inhales. "Ejection
fraction" for how much the heart spits out.

Where's her laundry basket? Pick up the dropped,
take a step, pick up more dropped, repeat. The lift
chair, bought to protect and assist, turns evil when
she fiddles with the controls, bruises her head, can't
sleep for two days. Still recognizes the Irish sweater
she knit me. What she has lost: writing, walking,
most talking, rolling over in bed, dialing, cutting
food, reaching the mouth, counting back by sevens.
Not chewing. Not the president, the day of the week,
the difference between me and my kids. Not laughing.
Not yet.

I'd want more than the weekly drive to the friend
or the doctor, the daily phone call. I fear four rooms
of valuables, banks, taxes, mourning work looming.
But I love my daughter more for her crayoning kindness,
my husband more for heaving the wheelchair gently up
into our house for a birthday dinner. And then Mom
sings into the phone "You Are My Sunshine," whole
first verse, no reason. I had hoped to understand more
by the end. Maybe that's enough.

What Is Metempsychosis?

At death, the soul moves into the body of an animal.
Perhaps the earth owns a fixed number of souls.
A pair of plumbers dreamt they had been peacocks.
In German: *seelenwanderung*. Sounds less crazy.

Gautama transmigrated five hundred and fifty times.
A bad guy became a broomstick. I was mere dirt,
then the soil isotopes in a bird's wing, later the bird.

Imagine the soul jumping into the kitten jumping
after the rabbit's foot. Imagine the naughty dog's soul
running in his sleep, dying into the footless rabbit.

And then, the lightning bug on a Ferris wheel.
I became the best man from my worst wedding.
I came back as the Amish girl named "Amen," but
I was happiest as the small-town cow. Now, this.

Help. My Mother Is Dead. I Feel Light.

She lived two years in a falling spark.

My social mother, hostess of the forty-year
Christmas Tea, ladylike but loving a raunchy
joke, was reduced to a whispered *ssss* for yes.

The mourning-her-alive poinsettia,
yellow and spindly, drops its leaves.

Help, my mother is dead, and so I should
be flailing, and miserable, but a weight
has lifted, replaced by a red sash of guilt.

No longer watching for each medical mistake,
monitoring the wound for increased redness,
which appears only late Fridays, ER the only option.

No longer struggling to cover her stiff arms,
praying like a dead ant's. When she held
her cheek, how could I know if she was in pain?
Surely she was when that tooth fell out?

Parkinsheimer's or whatever it was
snatched her from my children, who had gleefully
ganged up with her against me.

As if the mantra, talk as if she could understand, not
knowing if she was bored or miserable or done,
dying an inch a day. It could be worse, I said for months,
knowing it would be, and was. Can I skip ahead please?

Then, ghostwriting her Christmas card from hospice.
Then, the chilling one-note teeth grinding, each night.

Did she simply recede into beforetimes,
a four-month-old without the crying? Could
she cry? Would she? She hadn't much before,
was proud of that.

The last day, Christmas Eve, she couldn't blink.
At 1 p.m. I asked the nurse for eye drops.
She said we'd need a prescription.

Years ago, right after Dad died, I'd traveled for work,
called home every day. Her beloved six-toed cat,
cranky Hobbes, was failing—her last animal.

Every day I asked, "How's Hobbes?" "About the same."
When I came home, he was long dead. She hadn't lied.
"About the same," "dead," close enough for her.

She'd protected my mood, even then, when
I might have been able to comfort her.
Even then, she wished me light.

All the Birds Now Silent in the Yard

When was the last time she sat outside before she died?
Was that the year the birds didn't come,
and then another year? And then the rest.

The mourning dove mated for life, milky song
like the sun sliding down a web across a trail.

The music of warm coins in a pocket?
The thrush sounded like that, if the coins were gold.

For cowbird, serial birth mother laying chicks in other nests,
imagine one water drop from a cave's high ceiling.

Eagles should've sounded like red-tailed hawks,
which screeched like guts snapped out of fresh kill.
Instead, a squeaky keyboard space bar falling down the stairs.

One owl hollered a stuttering siren descending.
That rusty swing in the distance? Reminiscent of blue jay.

There was a sparrow with a voice like a Ping-Pong ball settled by a paddle.
You're familiar with tribute bands? The mockingbird was the avian equivalent.

I do not miss Canada geese. Their hostile hiss-knell
rattled, the expired pain pills of the dead.

Mom had always wanted a wren to weave her hair from the brush
into its nest. We didn't remember to try that in time.

Now we're left with the nagging squirrel like a scolding crow,
twitching its tail at twice empty air.

All through the Longest Night

They must have been buried in the road,
my dead, as I think of them when I leave
and come home. Their smells fade, voices dim.
Orion forever reminds me of Dad, dead in December.

Will the sky always taunt me with loss?
They must have been buried in the wind,
my dead. The grasses move like his fur did,
my pup, my Jesus-in-a-dog-suit, standing guard

as I learned to camp alone, after the first marriage
ended and I refused to stay away from the woods.

My mantel fills up with my late beloveds.
I think of them jammed down there in the dark,
their old-school virtues rusting and rarer now.
Later, their photos will sink in boxes or landfills.

With tilt of axis and passage of hours, more
dazzling days, less darkness, other constellations
rise. The road can be driven, the wind plays again,
drops death for a while. We retell the stories.

There is dark lively light, flashes on gravestones
from passing high beams, and bright lively light,
fire the juggler twirls, rising up from the frigid,
fertile waters, of the Sound, on the solstice.

3.

The Mutual Gratitude of Fountain and Solstice

after Pattiann Rogers's "The Importance of the Whale in the Field of Iris"

They would be hard to tell apart,
   except for the deep pendulum
between the throwing and falling,
   and the juggling globes of shine.

Indistinguishable, except
   for the way one draws celebrants,
and the other slices us into
   the fireworks of before and after.

One counts the wrens feeding their chicks
   and geese leaving the pond's silk face,
and divides by two. One subtracts
   the blooming from the hailing, then

adds flotsam's jetsam, shakes, then stirs.
   Both will offer you front row seats,
praise goosebumps under terry cloth,
   hijack you in whirlpooling

growing and dying—marry you.
   Solstice: yet-unblown dandelion.
Fountain: tiara worn deep in
   the Junest moonlit ballroom night.

If you didn't see them dancing,
   you'd think one paints with coolest mist
and hot sidewalk, and one baby steps
   with your approaching-sometime death.

They teeter at the apex, sun's
   closest moment, fountain's dark side,
precise in their swirl of dandle-
   down glitter, inseparable.

World Premier, Nocturnal Bird Migration Concert

Metro Assignment, Prospect Park, Brooklyn

On high highways of wind, three to five billion
birds head north for the summer, sometimes
singing, calling through fog, short *tseeps*
hard to distinguish, impossible to ignore.

Focus your spotting scope on the full moon
to see them whiz by, but that's like watching
baseball through binoculars locked at first base.
They appear, tiny dots, benevolent squalls

on Doppler radar if you know how to look.
Why bother seeing a four-inch finch 500 feet up,
when the clamor, everywhere, reaches for miles?
Why not just listen, past midnight, past words?

The sounds form their own cartography.
If you're an hour north of a lake, you'll hear
birds for an hour, then a lake-shaped, hour-shaped
silence, since few birds depart from water,

then raucous hellos from the southern shore.
Listening, hearing: acts of fond hope.

Epithalamion for Jesus and the Springfield Community Church

for the marriage of the Lamb has come, and his Bride has made herself ready.

—Revelation 19:7

Dressed in fine linen, bright and pure, they stepped up to the altar,
whispered their vows, enjoyed ambrosia salad, crispy fried meat loaf.

She treasured a rare snapshot of him holding a puppy, not a lamb.
He loved how quickly she volunteered to staff the nursery and to bake.

The two become one flesh at that long table, on line making lunch,
Wonder bread, bologna, cheese, mayo, lettuce, to feed the homeless.

One flesh at the midnight service, joining in centuries-old song.
One flesh by the grave, warm hands on the mourners' backs. But, and,

poems about long marriages that don't have *but*s in them are lies.
A marriage's first frost: the wedding ring dermatitis, the Bride's favorite

hymn sung too slow, the Lamb's sermon missing a single revelation.
The elders can't stomach bare shoulders at the eight o'clock service.

Tithes decrease, and children cuss. Still. Years ahead, some come
back carrying infants, psalms their balm, up front steps worn from use.

Trains Running after Storms

headline, The New York Times, *July 20, 1997*

I had to commit flight.
I had seen too many birds escaping, flying
off to the sides, as if I were evil. In the east the rumbling
called to me, kept ahead of me, vanished.
I rose and laughed.

"Be confident," the other trains told me. "Rise wildly."

I saw a star that appeared for only a second.
Then another star, then another. Short, fast stars.

All far more complex than we had imagined:
the sky, the flat land, the fields. There is more so of everything,
like daybreak in a house you knew first at night.

In one car everyone had the same name,
all the Yolanda Schmidts on the planet at once.

I saw meteors all day behind the sunlight.

Yolanda, age nine, wanted to know what *never mind* really means.

The fields near Spokane look like lily pads,
green circles of irrigation systems.

The last train followed the last engine, like the flung-back droop
of columbine spurs, triumphant. We were magnificent.

"We're in the castle of the angels!" the five-year-old Yolanda hollered.

You know the look of the small plane flying beneath the big plane,
that sliding lack of control?

Perhaps this is a forever-night-stand, the 37-year-old Yolanda thought,
pondering what had happened very early this morning.

Have you ever seen a bee land on a bud
and both fall fast to the ground?

When we land, there's a tunnel in the moon.

Her Thoughts That October

She wanted to paint his portrait, an ultimate gift of attention.

She wanted to paint
    how he looked to himself in the shiny panel
        of elevator buttons;
    how he looked to himself in the glass
        over the Klee at the Modern;
    how he looked to himself in the water fountain chrome as he drank.

She wanted to paint him from the neck down, waiting,
    holding one elbow, all housewifely
        in the dryer window.

She wanted to paint this man on hold,
    and his factual look as they cut his hair,
        his sweet courage, giving blood.

She wanted to paint his eyes done crying, red-rimmed, green,
    to paint what she saw during their kiss,
        his self become one light point.

Then she would teach him to paint himself.
The portrait would show his increasing
satisfaction as the resemblance grew.
He would have to keep changing it.

While he worked, she painted him
    touching the paintbrush to a mirror,
        including there, the ever-present shadow of her nose.

I Am the Sexy Museum

Within me, scurry from hall to hall.
No more slow walking the sandstone edifice
with marble floors that exhaust the feet.

Who needs portraits of bored people? Why galleries full
of empty landscapes, of war heroes on horses, when men
think about sex nineteen times a day, women ten?

Bring me airbrushing and alabaster, mastery of aperture,
harlequins in flagrante, every kind of specific exposure,
art from top and bottom POV, a hall of mirrors—

on ceiling, on headboard, at foot of bed. Cubists
are welcome—*Penetration of Guitar in Blue*—
Bosch is invited, and any pointillist who can

replicate a delicate, hectic touch. Pollock clearly
got it, kept his juices flowing. Who doesn't
prefer the pulsing life to the still one? Enter

a salon for frottage, the vigorous rubbing
both of pencil on paper covering leaf or coin,
and of stranger by stranger in subway car.

The special traveling photo exhibit features
couplings by the light under the door, a soul
two points of brightness. Enjoy my sculpture garden

featuring Brancusi's marital aids, Noguchi's dreams, loggia
of fellatio, the world's first gallery containing only art
inspired by the desire for older women. Containing, but barely.

How You Meet the Year Is How You Spend the Year

Winthrop, Washington

In one of its truer announcements,
the narrator's voice in my head said:
This is me.

Here in this dry sunny valley, cross-country skiing
on a perfect trail, I felt a bolt slip into place,
a puzzle piece, a center.

This wide basin, five hours from the city,
the valley of houses miles apart in the rolling scrub,
is my tap of the conductor's baton on the music stand,

the smell of a new piece of paper, the sound of a soda can
opening, a bite of iceberg lettuce, but only if one thinks
of iceberg lettuce as crisp and wet and clean.

Each square foot of snow has shining facets in seven colors, a windfall.
It didn't have to be this way. Snowflakes could've been dull, or each flake
could glow like a pearl. Long white pine needles sip light from above and below.

In the cabin a Russian climber wakes us strumming classical guitar music
and delivering coffee to each sleeping bag. Also here, a strong, strong woman,
my friend, raised feral in Alaska, expecting her first child, naps through the banter,

a tiny being nested inside her, in deeper sleep, in a warm cabin in a freezing valley.
Our hostess plays the flute; her friend made two tater pies, dessert and breakfast.
Oleg told us at midnight, *"Kak vstretish, tak evo i provedyosh,"*

how you meet the year is how you spend the year.
How lucky if that means with friends, the lovely world,
the narrator speaking clearly of who I am, and where.

Map, Lewiston, Idaho, June, 1933

Here there are friends
here the locks are easily opened
here nobody lives
here there's a lot of money, but carefully hidden

here lives a woman alone

here people regard gypsies as thieves
here live greedy people, but easy to steal from
here lives a man with a bad temper
here live scared people

but here lives a kind woman

here there is nothing of any interest
here there is nothing to be afraid of, go on begging
here they demand that you work hard
here are watchful neighbors

here lives only a mistress with maids

here are dogs in the yard, watch out!
here people tell you to go to hell
here they'll rough you up
here they take revenge

here they'll take care of you if you are ill

here they give no money but you may get food
here they give you food if you work
here they give only if you are ill
here they give nothing

and here you can get whatever you want.

A Dozen Secrets from God

A baby giggles, on average, 400 times a day.

I can help you add sand to your hourglass.

Church has gotten me wrong.

Think of me more as the cutest thing possible,
as if your all-time favorite dogs time-traveled and had a puppy,
and raising me gently is your only job.

I am the one exclamation point hidden in your encyclopedia.

In my next universe, hummingbirds will sound like thumb pianos.

I am that fountain you didn't have time to visit
at the hilltop castle garden, and you probably won't be back,
but you remember it more clearly than if you had thrown coins in.

Caution: low flying owls, and expectations.

Count how often each year you let rain fall on your face.

When your dog is listening to you, he's not frustrated.
He doesn't wish he knew what you are saying. You sound to him
the way birds sound to you. You're simply chirping.

The stars are just glints shining through a blurry lens;

I am the big thing shining behind.

And you, you are wine for the eyes.

Found, from My Daughter

Do years come back?
Can you wear lava?
Can you drink lava?
Is there a round river?

Is lightning upside-down or right-side up?
Does Addie miss us in heaven?
Do cows get married?
Is the sun alive?

I'm touching God. And the year.
I love you so dumb much.
The cardinal sounds like a tambourine.
I love you too much for you to die.

Can you build the world? Out of bricks?
What's the air made of? How do eyeballs see?
Can you have blue-green hair?
Won't you be my garden?

He hit me, and it's do unto others
as you would have others do unto you.
So he wants me to hit him.
I am as clean as a daisy.

I am as warm as a daisy.
Let's call the cat Dissa-monga-nofus
When is God's birthday?
Do any birds eat leaves?

Is the ocean an animal?
Why is one first?

4.

"Would You Learn Your Lesson If I Made You Take Your Clothes Off?"

She turned in the found purse to the police, because it was the right thing to do.
Even a recent newcomer from San Salvador would know that.
And coming from San Salvador, she also knew exactly why the cop came by
the next day, and called the day after, and for weeks after that, even when Carlos
complained, even when she complained. It stopped eventually. Until the night
she filled up her car on the Hempstead Turnpike, and there was his cruiser.
He threatened trouble. There were still questions about how she found the purse.
She should follow him in her car. She did. The woods were empty; he forced her in.

A blow job is the easiest sexual act to do poorly—the tenderest part
of the man meets the strongest muscle, the sharpest part of the woman.

What would stop her from biting, shaking her head in terrier fury?

The gun. The language barrier. The fear.
Long Island cops choose their victims for vulnerability,
not for nerve. They choose immigrants, paroled chicks
who don't want to lose their licenses, ladies driving alone
at 3:45 a.m. after having the couple drinks they'll admit to,
a waitress sleeping in a car after a fight with her husband, single moms
who can't go to jail, women in beater cars from beater neighborhoods.
Women who don't mutilate patrol officers. More's the pity.

As we were walking into county police headquarters, carrying notebooks,
past all the news trucks, up to where the small man with the crew cut stands
in front of the microphones and the Great Seal of the County of Nassau,
some cop says to me, "Wow, it must be a really slow news day."

"See Something, Say Something"

Penn Station

Suspect commuters. Hundreds of them.
National Guard guys whose camo doesn't work,
it needs to be neon or fast-food yellow-and-red
or pinstripe or Burberry plaid. Krispy Kreme.
Guy rooting his wiggly pinky deep into his ear.
Bookstore. Knobby man in pink tutu, on a dare
or coming out. Black kid perching on a backpack,
looking. Hudson News. Angry career women
in stilettos with no one to rub their feet at night.
Officer, I see a pregnant woman. Old guy sitting
beneath a gray smudge on the wall, halo of hair oil
and grime. Always here. Kicked cigarette butt
skittering like a rat. German shepherd with nothing
it wants to sniff. Crowd pulled from every direction
to four doors, fast. Lady hoisting a stroller upstairs,
guy, passing her glare, muttering, "It ain't *my*
fuckin' kid." A yawp and a man shuffling, no socks.
Ninety business sections in the trash. Same stockings
on mannequin legs for the last fifteen years. Rifles
of Guardsmen. No unattended packages. Every day

I forget to be very afraid.

Notes from a Survey of Home Health Aides

We'd meet at the East Orange Dunkin' Donuts, pink and orange
hard plastic chairs, trays basking under fluorescents. A snack
for answers to the writer's many questions. Half on food stamps,
$10 an hour, no raise in years. Wish I'd offered real food.

"I'm drained. The agency doesn't give me the hours. Can't live on 20."
"Millie chews on her fingers till they bleed, even on the way home
from the doctor." "My lady wakes me up every 10 minutes.
She pays me for 24 hours, wants me to work all 24."

exhausting, even the choices, Dutch apple, strawberry, Boston kreme

"This man now, he hits me. He calls me nasty names, has old timers,
chases me around the table. Boss says I have to give two weeks' notice.
The social worker says call 911. I gotta eat. His daughter doesn't say hi
when she comes in, doesn't even notice there's another person here."

glazed blueberry, chocolate crumb cake, cruller, sour cream

"One lady played with her poo. They call it *scatolia*, sounds pretty but, no.
She woke me, patting my face with her dirty hands." "I'm 68 and I'll do this
for as long as I can, until I need me an aide." "She threw out my dentures.
They were on the sink. It's $300 to replace them, so I just won't."

frosted with sprinkles, cider, butternut, chocolate peanut butter cream

"This other aide does it all wrong, puts the whites with the darks
and things go missing. The son gets up in my face, asking who'd steal
a widow's wedding ring? Have you met me? When she dies, I'll cry
more than him. I swore I'd do this work if God spared *my* ma years ago."

"They don't pay me to drive to each house. My engine gave out, so I work
where I can take buses. I don't see my kids much, but they're OK."
"When I first changed a man's diaper, I threw up. Next day I prayed
to make it through." "Just coffee please. I haven't been sleeping well lately."

Looking at *Saint Francis in the Desert*, Two Days before War

Today at work they trained us
in dozens of blistering ways to die,
how to run from smells of almonds,
geraniums, fresh-cut grass,
how we need to be lucky all our lives
but terrorists need luck just once.
The best way to leave a room fast?
Skirt the walls. Don't run straight.
Now that we all know this, we can
run into each other along the walls.
And the gas masks and protective suits
aren't available, last only three hours anyway—
and do you really want a suit if the only way
to relieve yourself is down into your boots?
Yes you do, or else you die, or so they say.

And what if this gallery were empty for 200 years,
a dirty bomb's half-life? St. Francis would still
stare to the left, up and holy, presenting his heart
to the light, slack, awed, without his self, with bliss.
His hands open beside him, à la garden statue,
though no bird lights on them yet. The canvas shines,
tiny sparks in the daylight sky, glamorous, real.

The room smells of grandmotherly upholstery.
The canvas's wormholes were filled in 1928.
A guard paces slowly. A rabbit looks at the artist.

Whatever the saint contemplates, I see the opposite. In his spring,
the donkey stands beneficent, the desert blooms, the wounds
appear out of adulation and empathy. We will run, perhaps
bleed out, if we smell that garlic in the grass.

"Louis Wore His Beeper in His Coffin"

Pete, 16, "Fashions for the Dead," Camden County Youth Center

"He was cool. He always wore his beeper,
waiting to hear from girls." Along the route
to the burial, small branches show that color
that reminds me of palest green spray paint.

Fire truck's on fire, police in handcuffs.
Camden has no movie theater, no groceries,
but dollar stores, but go-go bars. Nana
raised him. She has gray lashes, beat eyes.

The scanner said, "West district units directed
to BOLO for this juvenile," be on look out.
The face looked young but was not young,
stained by close-held tears and doubt,

like the old pillow under the pillowcase.
You leave behind the empty cold highway
in front of the ten-car pileup, blank.
You live outside our schedule, daily day.

What will you do all morning, all night?
The space behind your brow zero, blank,
blind like dolls thrown down, silent.
Eyes closed always. Blind. Deaf. Dank.

Batterles done, buried under klieg lights
in the cemetery next to Highway 132,
a jack-in-the-box folded down and in.
Who's trying to reach you now, Lou?

Deserted Trail off the Mountain Loop Highway

Three miles below the trailhead, the road sinks, in a chassis-bending gouge.
The Forest Service hasn't fixed it. The sign's askew, salted by shot,
Pinnacle Lake Trailhead, lead pellets indicating You Are Here.

No boots have swept the path. Needles rest in contour maps,
dark and thick where snow melted from beneath them.
Spider webs, tiny traps, appall and annoy the face.

The air is a lotion. Skin smells of pine.
The trail veers off and dead-ends, veers off,
dead-ends. Bring a map, compass, bug spray, patience.

    The hiker who found them, up on the right, wondered
    at first, were they picnicking, napping? No, bleeding
    from holes. Cold to the touch. Too many bottle flies.

Tendons of fir roots stretch across the path in Vermeer light.
A varied thrush, its distant sleighbell song of minor fifths,
asks, answers. A single raven hunts through the valley.

In Snohomish County jails the sheriff gave away playing cards,
each printed with an old murder, to help the memory of snitches.
Mary Cooper and Suzanna Stodden, mother, daughter, ace of hearts.

"I would go to a remote area that's not anywhere near where you live,"
a serial killer, not theirs, told cops before stabbing his wrist with a razor blade.
"I would let them come to me in a remote area." Eleven years later, case still cold.

    The hiker clutched his ice ax, raced back to his car,
    wondering who watched from the woods, who might follow
    with bullets. For two miles he heard nothing but his heart.

Monastery for the Modern Journalist

I am done
and ready to be
more useful.

I can no longer stand the breastbones of purple martins
protruding skyward from trembling breasts as they lie
dying from pesticides.

And while I know in theory it is important to ask the mother
about her stabbed son, "so people can understand what was lost here,"
I let her walk by, folded over, uninterrupted.

I can't place another call to widows of bond traders and firefighters
and hear how Daddy would pick up the boy and play him
like a banjo, but Mom isn't strong enough now.

I have sought this quiet room, where no wires enter,
none leave. No cell service, just a cell,
a cot with faded cotton blankets, a bureau
with two drawers. One candle.

I remember, quietly, and request:
Something, who knows what,
for the municipal landfills left to leach
when capping them is too expensive.

Something, God alone knows,
for the ten-year-old, who, when
undressed for examination, kicks her legs apart
stiffly, as a stepfather taught her years ago.

A scrubber of carbon, a reviver of bees,
the reinvention of the dusky sparrow,
a nobler motive than profit, and bountiful
schools for everyone, to nurture each child's gift.

That would be a start. Almost enough
to draw me back to write those stories.
And suggest a thousand more.

Watching All the Way Home from a Tough Interview, Seat 28A

L.A.'s a giant microchip, a much of muchness,
no green or shade, what 3.8 million of us look like,
then, below, desert, gray dust, my source's prospects.

Slowly, hills, trees, a high basin and west-facing cliffs,
red-tinged like a canyon, the place I'd land given
the coordinates. How big are those farm fields

and why? Cars move like minutes, and Biebl's
"Ave Maria," *a capella* over the tiny whiskey,
glides, a songworm soundtrack. Down there

lie well-worn places where folk songs are true.
Moon-colored horse, voters for those other
candidates, a barn a stunning cardinal flower,

legato. Still others in prisons, alternate lives.
That other paper that offered to hire me,
where I live in a brick house painted white,

where I got into grad school and married
that guy in Michigan, had too many kids,
and learned to cook well. Over there, look,

maybe a hearse on its way to a funeral
with no cars behind it with lights on;
outbuildings in Indiana-ish; a farmed

island in Lake Erie; a restroom break
over Ohio; and six minutes total cloud cover.
Why so clear? East, an acceleration of clutter,

scars in the Pennsylvania trees, from roads
overgrown in the woods? Subdivisions?
After the pilot said we were 75 miles west

of Newark, I saw those odd Pocono ski slopes,
the corporate headquarters I grew up near,
yes the church where I was baptized and married.

I wonder what will I see as I drift down to sleep,
light-jewels on velvet earth, houses, luck, dear
bodies sleeping, parallel, perpendicular? Home.

5.

Three Endings

Dying, see colored lights in a shabby city,
think of darkness, mourn next Christmas.
Friends surround you with food, books,
songs, touch. The new fellowship, over-
due, leaves you more homesick for life.

Minnow hooked through mouth and gill, pole resting
in the holder, boat zipping to the next hole, brilliant
spray, gleeful speed, guide's friendly chatter, fish
bouncing through glitter still writhes when we stop.

Each year in India, three hundred nine thousand
three hundred babies a year die in their first day.
Make words for a song for the babyless mother,

shunned, bewitched. And words for another song,
soul spending seven hours in this wondrous world.

Do not give her a name. Dig a grave a foot long.

Theme and Variations

Maybe the existence of divinity in the universe depends in part on us. We may be the consciousness of the universe, the way by which it can come to see and love and honor itself. If this is so, then our obligations are mighty and humbling. We are cocreators. We are servants.

—*Pattiann Rogers, "Surprised by the Sacred"*

I.
The Christmas pageant featured something new
at least to me: a real live infant. St. Peter's had used a lightbulb
in the manger. I'd had to kneel and stare at it, hands in prayer,
when I was the littlest angel, five and underlit by gleaming
electric holiness. Other pageants used sad once-a-year dolls,
faces smudged by unloving thumbs. So when a pre-teen Mary
carried this little guy in, slung over her curveless hip, held
safely but not maternally by one elbow, one knee, my eyes
welled up, for some reason unconnected to my thoughts. Yes,
Jesus was real, like our toddler, who's old enough to understand,
though not old enough for church. At home, I told her and her father
about the real baby Jesus, and she mimicked me, raising her arms
like the holy rollers we are not, and said, "It was a real baby."

II.
For 16 years Robert Evans searched the night for supernovas, finding
a blink in the sky about every six months. There's something satisfying,
he said, in thinking of light on its travels through space for millions of years,
then at the single moment it hits our planet, someone looks up in one tiny
circle of sky, noticing: "It just seems right that an event of that magnitude
should be witnessed." Despite similar odds, we find our correct husbands.
Our children are born healthy. We make it home from work. We create
a world. But we can keep it—knock wood—only if we love it.

III.
If I hear profound music, the men's choir at midnight, or that resonant
trumpet Ben practiced in the high school stairwell, and if I close my eyes,
I join with wordless purity, feel a part of myself rising into a huge uprushing,

my droplet evaporating gladly to the sun. I'm at the edge of a giant column,
a spirit quietly roaring up through the wall of an immense artery,
on the rim with the others in the state fair Spin-a-Tron,
the planet's centrifuge. I jump.
The high note is perfect.
I serve.

Please Bring a Moon

Kate loves the moon. I carry her,
she throws her head back and tilts up
her chin to watch. I see its reflection
in her perfect new eyes.

She holds her hand up in greeting.
This reminds me how the moon's
its own cocoon, how hard it is
to explain, how the world

would manage perfectly fine without
it and its changes, its hiding in clouds,
its two-week disappearances, awfully
long when you're a year old.

I used to count each new crescent
as a step closer to her birth. I used to
know where End of the Moon Lane is.
I once saw two owls flying across a field

on the full moon, and a few minutes later,
a feather floating down from the sky.
I caught it. I will tell her, but will she tell
her child? What would a baby moon

be called, moonlet, moonling, and how
would it hatch? Will she watch it
from the back seat, a constant with trees
passing through like thread?

On Successfully Becoming Invisible in My Own Home

I'm balled up, a giant seed behind the hamper of mittens
in the closet under the stairs, obscured by long coats.

The spawns run up and down overhead,
thundering like a war
in an adjoining theater,
looking for me.

I have the afternoon's best spot.
I almost laugh aloud
when one kicks the hamper,

peeks in quickly, groans, shuts
the door, and runs to the basement,
leaving me with the sounds of my skull,
the furnace-sounding blood, the breath
suddenly here, though ever here.

They are hollering Ma!
as if I would answer.

But how would they sound if I never came out,
if "olly-olly-oxen-free" lost its magic, if I were
truly gone for good but not for *good*?

I'd become the bright round awareness
flitting through the house like the spotlight
bouncing off the guitar at the coffee house,
stroking their faces, mistaken for glare.

I'd nest in the upper corner of their rooms
after they had fully fallen down the sleepstairs
and their breath shushed to distant surf.

Or maybe I'd stay in the leather smell of closet,
left over from their late grandfather, so loved.

From this spot, I could hear the breakfast
battles, the menu planning, the playdates
months after the funeral luncheon, and the wailing
into towels about Mommy never coming back.
Not for Christmas like Frosty. Not ever.

What's in the taste that makes things stale?
A bit of mold, a bit of dirt, plus the cellar plus time.
A box of photos got tossed by the movers. The journals
were lost when the garage burned down. She forgets
my voice. He forgets how the smell of my shirts
used to remind him of nursing. She forgets that my ruby ring
was a gift from Pa for my second wedding. She forgets
that ruby ring at a sorority party sink.

We'd agreed their dad could remarry after the ink
was five years' dry on the death certificate.
He chooses someone two cup sizes larger.
They will all move to a smaller place, leaving
me here until a stranger sweeps me out.

But the slatted door swings open,
hall light wincing bright. I am found.
I am It. And they laugh so loudly
at how well I could just disappear.

On the Lackawaxen with Kate, 2008

Wading in the river with my seven-year-old daughter,
my usually obstreperous I-WON'T-brush-my-teeth girl,
I see her looking at me adoringly. How dear.
Engaged, winning, she likes me for once, this gorgeous day.

Then I realize, no, she is mugging at her reflection
in my sunglasses. I am merely a wall for her to bounce
herself off, a learning tool, an object she uses
to see herself, adore herself. I say "you're looking

all lovey-dovey at you, not at me!" We laugh together.
She replies, "The name Debbie gives me the impression
of a webbed foot stomping on a puddle." When Daddy
calls on his way to us that night, she tells him "I want

to sing you a kiss." All we can do is write it down,
and help her love herself for all the best reasons.

The Music of Places Going On without Us

Four times every minute the twelve-tonned sea
shoots a white fusetip of breaking wave north,
scrambling in a roar. Next the pounding through
the gorge resounds, the waterfall hitting rock slope,

splaying with white weight, loud yarn spilling,
at 5 a.m., noon, midnight. The heartbeat, rising gurgle
of stomach bubbles, guitar chords, muffled laughter,
singing of the national anthem, occasional sloppy-galoshes

of love: the womb. The storm coming up across the field:
road machinery? Hail. The maternal nag of hangers pushed
across the closet bar in the hot upstairs. Cicadas, their nightmare
noise closer to the brain than the sound of swallowing,

all erased by the cymbalcrash of diving into the pool. All
go on somewhere now. "Dixie" possesses the pipe organ
daily in Luray Caverns for tourists hundreds of feet underfoot.
The cat who ran away is purring somewhere, maybe.

Buzz of fluorescent lights eats through the library,
invading brains, a burrowing worm. People hear themselves
chewing lobster tails at our seaside bistro in Galveston.
The squeak of foot on floorboard (ceiling) announces nightfall

to the new renter in my old West Side apartment.
Every neighborhood has a three-year-old with a chimey
voice, her flipflops spreading their rickety rackety emily fidgety
riff. And in mountain towns sleet falls on sheds,

percussion for a small old song no one wrote down.
Last again is the waterfall, the skeined water unraveling,
no ends, no knots. And the snaredrumroll of ocean arcing
across the peninsula, reaching, always reaching, for the bay.

The Menopause Doula

Are your mother and aunts gone?
Friends facing their own symptoms—
irritability, empty nest, fatigue?
Men don't get it; kids don't care.
Perhaps I can meet your critical needs.

I will describe the 34 symptoms of the change,
the best being the end of menstruation, the rest
completely dreary—who would sign up for depression,
loss of libido, irregular odor, night sweats, dryness?
But truly, almost all are lessened by regular exercise.

I will show you the benefits of running early in the day.
It dusts the heart, polishes it with nourishing lemon oil.
Follow my advice, and I can nominate you for cover girl
of *My Menopause Magazine*. I can tell tales of women
who outsmart, start anew, and thrive. My services include:

commissioning a fine, sincere neighbor-man to mention you look hot;
foot rubs on demand—they give the same boost as a 30-minute nap;
a ten-page list of things you don't have to care about any longer:
what fruit your body's shaped like, what colors match your complexion,
Most Flattering Makeup Routines, who's on the cover of any magazine.

As one last introductory bonus, a few fun facts.
Climacteric, synonym for menopause, means critical period
or turning point. In fruit, it marks the peak of edible ripeness.
You're better at trivia having lived through more of it.
Universally, humans grow happier after age 51.

I can provide cool, damp cloths for the sudden 105-degree fever
that mugs you; a booklet of easy, new, nourishing, tasty recipes.
A lavender bath to erase the stale sweat. Sleep
masks, earplugs, melatonin, hand cream.
A partner in crying.

I will whisper to you, slowly,
over time, that invisibility
has privileges—at airport security,
at restrooms in diners where you're not
a paying customer, but no one cares.
And yes, in the mirror, the once-cranky mirror.

First Weekend Ever Home Alone

Usually our wrens sing like the aural equivalent of poplar leaves
shimmering in the wind—rococo, atwitter, too fabulous to transcribe.
That's the daylight song. The dawn song is a bossy shout, an adamant

anklegrab that leaves us with nothing to do but fret until the alarm
. . . will work let up, will the kids stop fighting, will those infernal birds . . .
but we don't want silence, really. We hung up the house on purpose.

Everyone I love enough to yell at is six hours north at the lake.
Work kept me here in detention, or blissfully alone, depending.
They took the dog. It would be far easier if they'd left him here.

So this is what widowhood almost resembles, this the empty nest, the mats
lying flat, perpendicular to the tub, one toothbrush neat on the counter.
I go four-hour stretches without talking, wake up afraid of noises.

These wrens fly as if battery-propelled, sprites ten times louder
per ounce than roosters. As the female approached the nest,
the male sang lookout. He distracted, encouraged.

A little bit ago, something turned their volume down.
They warned us with new rattlesnake scoldings. Here's why—
when they entered the birdhouse today, multiple squeaks,

like the smell of fresh air! I smiled. After an hour of feedings
and parental chirrings, sounding like a busy emery board,
the chicks, unlike children, quieted down. How many?

I have two, and they are spirited, interrupting, audacious,
energetic, exhausting, confounding, and hysterical, as in
funny, as in dramatic. I would, and do, bring them bugs all day.

In this my semi-perfect life, I have thankfully avoided infertility,
colic, autism, and many other nightmares. But I shudder thinking
of our friend's son's tumor, how unspeakably terrifying

to know something lethal grows inside a towhead. Time
and change are like that, just slower. I suspect that all joys, even
dishpan-brown, with a little schoolgirl plaid around the wings, end.

To Live: The Imperative

For all we know, though, ours may be the only planet in the universe hosting mind and consciousness. If so, then our decisions and our conduct will determine whether the universe has a long future as a conscious entity or will soon lapse back into unconsciousness.

—*Steve Stewart-Smith,* Darwin, God, and the Meaning of Life

There is a German verb, to separate souls from bodies.

How terrifying, the world without
the two bright lights
in our live, kind eyes.

Instead, a radiant glacier melts to black stone.

Maybe the universe reads all our email,
understands our jokes and work,
and loves our steel drums.

99% of all the species that ever lived are now extinct.

We counter with side curtain airbags,
programs to maintain brain health,
surefire weight loss diets.

A language dies every 14 days.

We bash ourselves upstream,
scraping flesh to find a mate.
Could you live in a world without fish?

What if fireflies stop blinking?

What does the sperm feel when
it wins? I praise the headlong
from love to egg and life.

40% of all humans ever died in their first year.

Each age loses sleep over air raids,
1984, Russia, Cuba, nuclear winter,
climate change, 2012, North Korea.

A quarter of our daughters are depressed or anxious.

The person I loved most in the world
went to solitude. He lives outside
my tenses. By now, you have felt this, too.

This is what hearing a hovering helicopter does to me.

There are stars so far away, their first light
has not yet reached us. We must remain,
the only ones to know and praise them.

Acknowledgments

I am indebted to the editors of the following publications in which these poems first appeared:

Adanna: "Monastery for the Modern Journalist"

Alaska Quarterly Review: "Getting Through the A's in *Angels: Their Names and Meanings*"

Battery Journal: "The Menopause Doula," "To Live: The Imperative," "Vitamin Awe," "What Is Metempsychosis?"

Blinders Journal: "How You Meet the Year Is How You Spend the Year," "Trains Running after Storms," "Watching My Father Watch His Widow"

Cimarron Review: "The Fetal Fawn inside the Roadkilled Deer"

Ekphrastic Review: "Looking at *Saint Francis in the Desert*, Two Days before War"

Journal of New Jersey Poets: "First Weekend Ever Home Alone," "The Hill Looks Steeper, the Two Maples Gone," "'I'm Having the Death I'd Always Hoped For,'" "Planting, Nearest the Prayer," "Theme and Variations"

Juxtaprose: "Watching All the Way Home from a Tough Interview, Seat 28A"

Midnight Oil: "Adding a New Heartbeat"

MER VOX: "I Am the Sexy Museum"

Mom Egg Review: "On the Lackawaxen with Kate, 2008"

North American Review: "Three Endings"

On the Seawall: "Map, Lewiston, Idaho, June 1933," "Please Bring a Moon"

One: "The Brother My Parents Almost Adopted," "I Wish You Had Known, When You Launched Me," "The Music of Places Going On without Us"

Paterson Literary Review: "World Premier, Nocturnal Bird Migration Concert"

Porter Gulch: "'Louis Wore His Beeper in His Coffin'"

Presence: A Journal of Catholic Poetry: "Epithalamion for Jesus and the Springfield Community Church"

TheRumpus.net: "Found, from My Daughter"

Shrew: "Looking at *Saint Francis in the Desert,* Two Days before War," "Notes from a Survey of Home Health Aides"

Terra Incognita: "Her Thoughts That October"

U City Review: "A Dozen Secrets from God," "The Dying in Slow Motion, The Woman Who Taught Me to Knit," "'See Something, Say Something'"

US 1 Worksheets: "The 87th Easter"

These poems appeared in the following chapbooks or anthologies:

Ardor: "Her Thoughts That October," "How You Meet the Year Is How You Spend the Year" (as "New Year's Day, Winthrop, Washington"), "The Music of Places Going On without Us," "Planting, Nearest the Prayer," "Theme and Variations," "Trains Running after Storms"

The Book of Donuts: "Why I Cried Reading This at Liss and James's Wedding"

Constellation of Kisses: "On a Record James Agee Recites from Memory His Poems, Auden's, Shakespeare's, Etc."

MetaLand: "'Would You Learn Your Lesson If I Made You Take Your Clothes Off?'"

Writers Resist Anthology: "All the Birds Now Silent in the Yard"

"The Music of Places Going On without Us" was nominated for a Pushcart Prize.

Pattiann Rogers's essay "Surprised by the Sacred" was first published in *U.S. Catholic*, with subsequent publications in *The Dream of the Marsh Wren: Writing as Reciprocal Creation*, published by Milkweed Editions (1999), and in *The Grand Array: Writings on Nature, Science, and Spirit*, published by Trinity University Press (2010). The quote on page 56 comes from *The Dream of the Marsh Wren*. Copyright © 1999 by Pattiann Rogers. Quoted by permission of Pattiann Rogers.

Steve Stewart-Williams's *Darwin, God, and the Meaning of Life* was published by Cambridge University Press (2010). Copyright © 2010 by Steve Stewart-Williams. Quoted by permission of Steve Stewart-Williams.

I am also indebted to the supportive and creative people at CavanKerry Press; to Baron Wormser and Joy Arbor, for inestimable help with the manuscript; to my writing workshop mates; and to my first readers, whom I adore unabashedly.

CavanKerry's Mission

A not-for-profit literary press serving art and community, CavanKerry is committed to expanding the reach of poetry and other fine literature to a general readership by publishing works that explore the emotional and psychological landscapes of everyday life, and to bringing that art to the underserved where they live, work, and receive services.

Other Books in the Emerging Voices Series

This book was printed on paper from responsible sources.